ON THE ROAD
JIMMIE JOHNSON

PHOTOGRAPHS BY

MISSY MCLAMB

ON THE ROAD
JIMMIE JOHNSON

Photographs by Missy McLamb

Published by Second Son Publishing
Brooklyn, New York

Design: Mark Pollard, Sylvia Weir, Steve Weir

ISBN: 978-0-615-658001

Second Edition; Printed October, 2012

Printed in the USA.

ON THE ROAD
JIMMIE JOHNSON

PHOTOGRAPHS BY

MISSY MCLAMB

ON THE ROAD, 2011

I don't know how I have survived watching my husband compete for a NASCAR championship eight years in a row. Of those eight years, Jimmie has won five titles. I never imagined that when I met him as a rookie, he would be going for an unprecedented sixth straight title in 2011.

This book portrays those ten weeks of The Chase that eventually led to the title going to Tony Stewart. Though the winning streak was over, it took an end for us all to look back and realize the magnitude of Jimmie's accomplishment.

We knew that win or lose this would be one of the biggest years of his career. Because of this, we wanted to document every step, not only for our family, but for those who wanted to see inside one of the sport's greatest competitors (in my loving opinion) on a quest for the ultimate. This book shows our family traveling across the country with our one-year-old Genevieve in tow. These pictures are a personal look into our life on the road and they will always take me back to a special time. We enjoyed the journey. I hope you do too.

THANK YOU TO OUR CREW, FRIENDS AND FAMILY FOR A GREAT YEAR!

Chandra Johnson

Chandra Johnson

22
TUMS
Sprint
NASCAR
LOWE'S
SIEMENS
SUNOCO
mylowes

THE CHASE

No one had ever won four-consecutive NASCAR championships, much less five.

In the fall of 2011, I was shooting for six in a row.

It's hard to slow down and grasp the meaning of that opportunity while you're doing it. My focus was winning No. 6—not the opportunity to win No. 6. As a NASCAR driver, I'm pulled in many different directions aside from my duties in the race car. I'm a spokesman for companies like Lowe's, Chevrolet, and many others. I'm a teammate to more than 500 employees at Hendrick Motorsports led by the best man in the business, Rick Hendrick.

And most importantly, I'm husband to Chani and father to Genevieve.

I'm always moving, going, doing. Winning a race feels amazing for a day or two. It is validation of the hard work we all put in, but the hard work never stops. It's on to the next race and the same goes for championships.

It is amazing when I look back and see how far I have come. Growing up in El Cajon, California, my life revolved around racing dirt bikes. Back then I was just a kid with big dreams.

Granted, I never dreamed I'd be in the position I am in now.

I was discussing this with a friend who'd achieved greatness in his sport, and he suggested I document the quest for six. He had once done so and years later really cherished it. Chani and I loved the idea and a week before The Chase hired our family photographer, Missy McLamb. She was a fresh eye to the sport and someone I was comfortable with being in my personal space, which made for some powerful images.

Ten weeks and 15,000 photographs later, we had documentation of the highest of highs and lowest of lows from my 2011 NASCAR Chase for the Sprint Cup.

We whittled those 15,000 images down to 200 behind-the-scenes photos of the sport, my team and my everyday life. This book is our journey in pictures.

WE HOPE YOU ENJOY IT!

Jimmie Johnson

48

GATORADE
48
Holley
USG
3M

Halfway through The Chase, (left) Victory Lane at Kansas Speedway.

My team celebrating our victory at Kansas Speedway.

SIMPSON
NASCAR

How Kansas Victory Lane looked from my vantage point.

Kansas Speedway

48
LOWE'S
4
17
2
29
16

Tearing up the lawn during my victory celebration at Kansas.

Jimmie Johnson
NASCAR RACE CAR
NASCAR Sprint CUP SERIES
Coors Light POLE
JEGS
48
TOOLS
TOP CHOICE
LUMBER PRODUCTS
www.bethematch.org

Rain delay at Homestead-Miami Speedway.

HOMESTEAD-MIAMI: RAIN DELAY & ENGINE TROUBLE

Heading into the final race of the season at Homestead-Miami Speedway, we did not have a shot to win a sixth-consecutive championship. But that did not mean there wasn't a goal. That has always been a strong-suit of the 48 team: we never settle, and constantly create obstacles to challenge ourselves.

In this race I'd hoped to finish well, and keep a different streak alive—finishing in the top 5 in the championship point standings for the 10th season in-a-row. But engine trouble prevented that and I ended the season sixth overall in the standings. It was tough to accept.

My walk to qualifying at Charlotte Motor Speedway (I'm talking my right foot into staying on the gas).

LOWE'S

LOWE'S
LOWE'S
Racing
Johnson

I'm not superstitious. I don't have a special pair of gloves, socks or underwear, but when it comes to setting an alarm clock or a timer, I always use the number 48 in it. Here I'm setting my alarm to the magic number.

One last shot before I roll out to practice in Martinsville.

A brief moment of downtime between pre-Chase events in Chicago.

LOWE'S

ERIC CARLE

My Girls. I'm a blessed man!

New Hampshire Motor Speedway Grandstands.

Taking a stroll through the Chicago motorhome lot with Genevieve.

Jimmie Johnson

KOBALT TOOLS
LOWE'S

GOODYEAR
GOODYEAR
EAGLE
3M
LOWE'S
LF

Charlotte Motor Speedway

Motorhome life.

I LOVE YOU

Home away from home—our motorhome kitchen.

K

Chandra and I walking the red carpet at the BeLive Gala in South Beach, a charity event held by our friends Connie and Juan Pablo Montoya to raise awareness of challenges in their home country of Columbia.

Following the BeLive Gala, we are headed to dinner in South Beach with our friend and fellow driver Brian Vickers.

Lowe's Racing
Jimmie Johnson
mylowes
ESPN

MARTINSVILLE SPEEDWAY

Martinsville Speedway and I will be linked forever. I've won a lot of races here, but suffered great loss, too. In 2004, a Hendrick Motorsports plane crashed on it's way to the race, and I lost many dear friends. I think of them every time I come back and miss them every day. On this day in the fall of 2011, I was again a favorite to win the race. But my championship was virtually over, after wrecking out at Charlotte.

I'm always respectful of my competitors on the track, and never want to jeopardize another driver's chance to race for a championship. Sometimes that respect goes too far. This was one of those times. I was battling Tony Stewart in the No. 14 car, a championship-contender, for the win. I gave him a lot of room on a late-race restart—probably more than I should have—and it cost me the win.

I knew I had let the win slip away and you can tell by my body language just how mad I am that I lost. It would have marked Hendrick Motorsports' 200th Cup Series victory as a company. Instead I had to watch Tony (Stewart) doing burnouts knowing that it should be me and all of HMS over there celebrating, especially at Martinsville, where HMS got their first win and where the tragedy happened.

"I TRIED TO BE SMART. THAT'S TYPICALLY HOW I RACE GUYS. I DON'T RUN OVER PEOPLE TO GET POSITIONS."

Chatting with the boss – Rick Hendrick.

Dover International Speedway

Lowe's Racing
Jimmie Johnson
LOWE'S

LOWE'S
LOWE'S
LOWE'S
Mechanix

Celebrating at Kansas Speedway.

Talladega Superspeedway

I traveled to Dallas, Texas to promote the upcoming 2011 Chase for the NASCAR Sprint Cup. I visited Byron Nelson High School and they held a Pep Rally in my honor. As you can see, it was a lot of fun. They rigged up this chair with two fire extinguishers and I raced the school principal and Eddie Gossage, Texas Motor Speedway president, from one end of the gym to the other. Wildest ride I've ever had on five wheels!

NASCAR
WE ARE
BOBCATS

Young fans enjoying Foundation Fest—a Jimmie Johnson Foundation event in Charlotte.

Hendrick
BOSCH
BOSCH
SIEMENS
SIEMENS

Media promotion prior to The Chase.

Hendrick
Racing

LOWE'S

CUP SERIES
LOWE'S
DELPHI
KOBALT TOOLS
TOP CHOICE
GOODYEAR
Jimmie
Johnson

MLB PLAYOFFS: THE COASTS ARE CLEAR
Sports
NASCAR'S DREAM
JIMMIE JOHNSON CRANKS
LOWE'S

Firesuits Dale Jr. and I wore during a commercial shoot for Time Warner Cable in Charlotte.

Sharing a laugh with Dale Jr. between takes.

Sprint

The 2012 Team Lowe's Racing photo shoot.

LOWE'S
Handrick
KOBALT TOOLS
TOP CHOICE

Doing an interview for ESPN from Victory Lane in Kansas.

Homeward bound.

Genevieve enjoying the ride home with Dad.

K

Preparing the BoDeans set list for Jimmie Jam Chicago.

Relaxing at a Jimmie Jam event.

On stage at Jimmie Jam Chicago with musician and friend Edwin McCain.

At the House of Blues Chicago.

On stage with Los Lobos. On my left is friend and driver Adrian Fernandez.

Chani is an Okie from Muskogee and an Oklahoma Sooner. Muskogee's former mayor, John Hammons, was one of the youngest mayors in America. He was first-elected at 19 years old! The Jimmie Johnson Foundation donates educational grants to three areas: my hometown of San Diego, Calif., Chani's hometown in Muskogee and our current residence, Charlotte, NC. We were in Muskogee for an event at one of the schools that received a grant and the Mayor gave Chani a key to the city in honor of her charity work there. (Right) Genevieve was enjoying playing a game of hide-and-seek behind the stage until curiosity got the best of her and she just had to look on stage to see what all the bright lights and noise was.

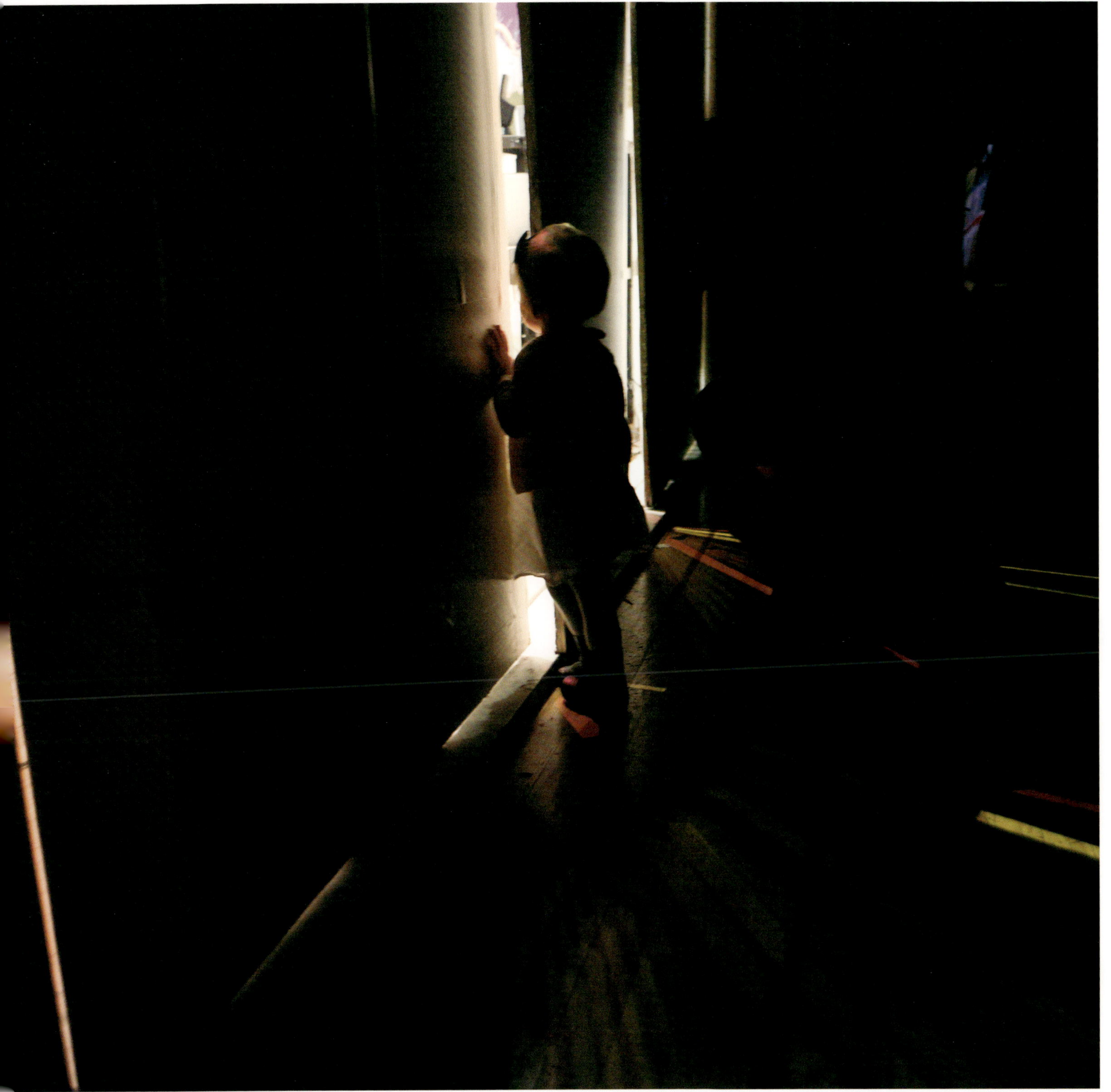

48
GOODYEAR

amp
88
Hendrick
KOBALT TOOLS
TOP CHOICE
LOWE'S
48
LOWE'S
Sprint
Sprint
STAGE
sprint.com/speed
STAGE

The smallest member of the crew.

The prerace prayer.

Homestead-Miami Speedway

Charlotte Motor Speedway

BOSTITCH
9
UPS Freight
6
KOBALT TOOLS

The Charlotte Motor Speedway crash.

48

POST CRASH

ANNOUNCER:
Whoa! Hang on there–Jimmie Johnson! Sideways!

ANNOUNCER:
Is he going to be able to save it? No.

ANNOUNCER:
No! What a hard hit.

RADIO:
We're done guys. We're in it.

ANNOUNCER:
That was a hard lick. Man. He was doing everything he could to try to save it.

ANNOUNCER:
Just what we've talked about all night. It's that air problem that you get, being that car on the inside, trying to make that pass. The five-time champ running 7th. With 17 laps to go. Looking like he was fighting that car and trying to get all he could.

ANNOUNCER:
He was gonna take the spot away from Newman, but the problem he had was the 4 car, Kasey Kahne was so fast coming from behind.

CHAD KNAUS:
Sorry fellows. That was my fault today.

ANNOUNCER:
You know I said that was the turning point of the race for the 48 team when they took those four tires. That's what he's talking about. It could be the turning point of The Chase for the 48 team.

ANNOUNCER:
No doubt about that.

ANNOUNCER:
That was a hard hit Jimmie Johnson just took, too. Hard hit.

ANNOUNCER:
You can see its affected Jimmie Johnson, too. He's trying to catch his breath right here.

ANNOUNCER:
The angle that he went in, the speed that he went into that wall. Thankful for all the safety equipment in these cars. The safer barrier that he hit. That was vicious.

This hurts. After the Charlotte crash I knew in my heart the chance for six-straight championships was over. I didn't quit, of course. I don't quit. Ever. But I knew. Watching it hurts, even today. This was the end of a very difficult week. The Charlotte crash happened on a Saturday night, and the next day I invited some friends to my house to watch the IndyCar finale on TV. My friend Dan Wheldon died in that race. Dan was a great person. He had such a big heart and it was so easy to get to know him that his death really hit me hard. He was in a similar stage of life that I'm in with a young family. His death was tragic and gave me perspective. Charlotte was tough to accept, but Dan's death put it in perspective.

LIONHEART

Dan Wheldon was special to me. I first met Dan when we were running the Rolex 24 hour event. He was easy to get to know and although we raced in different series, I really looked forward to seeing him and hanging out whenever our schedules had us in the same location. He was always very supportive of me and I was always pulling for him to do well.

So to pay tribute to him, I joined many other drivers in placing his trademark Lionheart decal on my helmet at Talladega. After the race I donated this helmet to an auction created by IndyCar driver Graham Rahal, to help raise money for Dan's family. I wanted to do whatever I could to help his widow, Susie, and their two young children. In the days after his death, tributes to him and footage of his wreck were on TV constantly. Chani and I are intently watching one of those tributes here. The looks on our face tell the story.

Watching news coverage of Wheldon's crash.

MID-OHIO SPORTS CAR COURSE
LEXINGTON, OH
DAYTONA200
my first words

Between practice runs at Phoenix International Raceway.

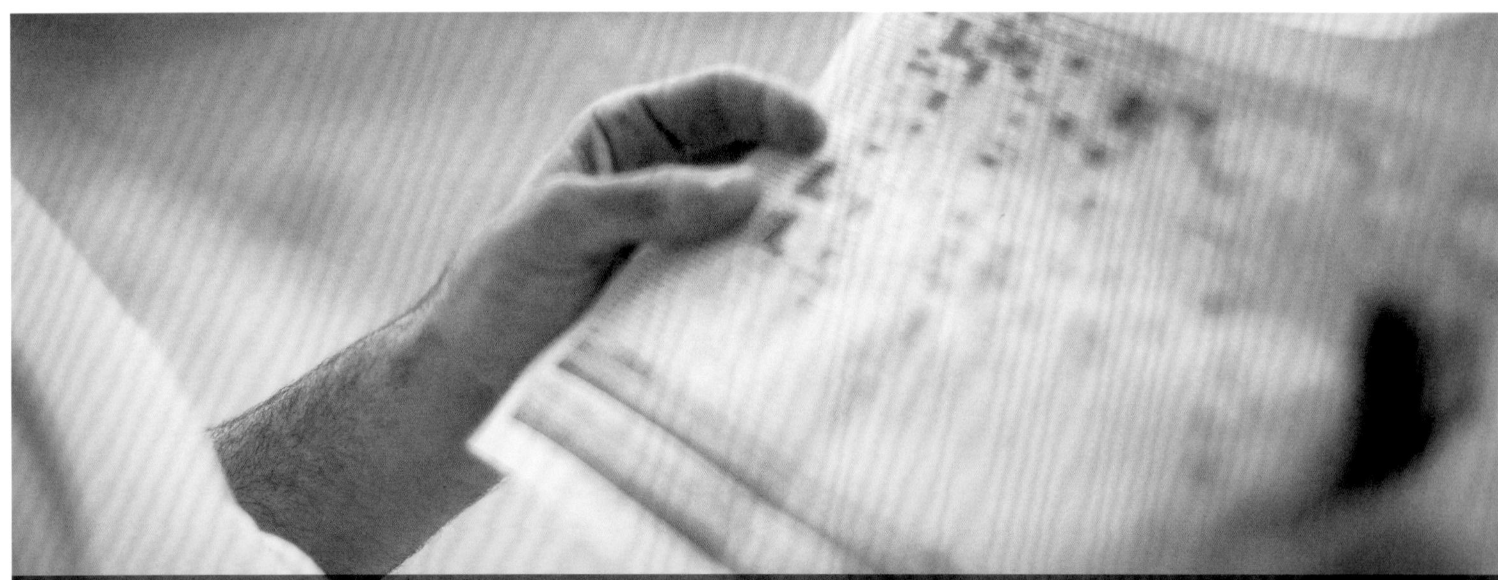

Every time I return to the transporter following a run on the racetrack during practice or qualifying, I fill out what we call an Outing Report. In this report, I explain in detail how the car reacted to certain changes we made to the setup. In this report there is a map of that week's racetrack to help explain exactly what I'm feeling and where. Another sheet we study during practice is called a Lap Tracker. It details every single lap made by every single racecar, then ranks them based on speed. The fastest are to the left, slowest to the right. These tools are important to gauge the competition and where we stand throughout each weekend.

Crew Chief Chad Knaus.

TP20

CUP SERIES
48
JOHNSON
IMPALA
Hendrick
MOUNTAIN DEW
79

R.E.
WE'S

48
LOWE'S
LOWE'S
DELPHI
GOODYEAR
SIEMENS
SIEMENS
BOSCH
LOWE'S

KOBALT
TOOLS
48
GOODYEAR
SUPPORT OUR TROOPS
www.bethematch.org
Holley
USG
3M
JEGS
LOWE'S
RR
(704) 652-8403

Phoenix International Raceway

CenterStage with Michael Kay, YES Network.

ESPN's NASCAR Now studio.

Production room of the YES Network.

On-set with Hannah Storm at ESPN's SportsCenter studio.

On my way to Late Night with Jimmy Fallon, New York City.

In the green room with Jimmy Fallon and my buddy, Doug Keith.

Late Night with Jimmy Fallon.

SONY

New Hampshire Motor Speedway

Strapping in for a practice run.

Chatting with Chad in the team transporter. His face tells me we are clearly not having a good day on the track.

TALLADEGA &
EASTABOGA BLVD.
CHECK-IN
GUEST SERVICES
OPEN 24 HOURS
SECURITY

Signing autographs on the way back to the transporter.

NASCAR
Hendrick MOTORSPORTS
NEXTEL
TEAM
LOWE'S
RACING
LOWE'S
DELPHI
LOWE'S
Let's Build Something Together

NASCAR fans

John Vignona, our motorhome driver, and Genevieve on our golf cart.

A fan at Talladega.

Talladega Superspeedway

A prayer at the end of a driver's meeting.

Talladega fans.

ALL WE
WANT
IS A WAVE
!!!

CLEARANCE
PRE-RACE
PIT ACCESS

Fans on the racetrack during driver introductions at Charlotte Motor Speedway.

This was a first for me: I was asked to Homecoming by a student during a pep rally at Bryan Nelson High School in Texas.

Loyal fans in any weather.

Pit road under caution at Texas Motor Speedway.

88
83
Red Bull

Crew getting the Lowe's Chevy ready for post race inspection.

NASCAR RACE CAR
Sprint CUP SERIES
MECHANIX WEAR
Holley HP CARBS
USG
3M
JEGS
GOODYEAR
EAGLE
Gatorback BELTS
MOOG CHASSIS PARTS
MAHLE
COMP CAMS
Edelbrock
SUNOCO
48
IMPALA

At Homestead-Miami during the rain delay talking to the crew guys.

The crew pushing the car to post race inspection at Texas Motor Speedway.

Phoenix International Raceway

Jimmie chatting with Car Chief, Ron Malec.

Pit road at Dover International Speedway.

New Hampshire Motor Speedway

The final restart at Kansas Speedway.

Prerace at Kansas Speedway.

Talladega Superspeedway

Stretching before the race.

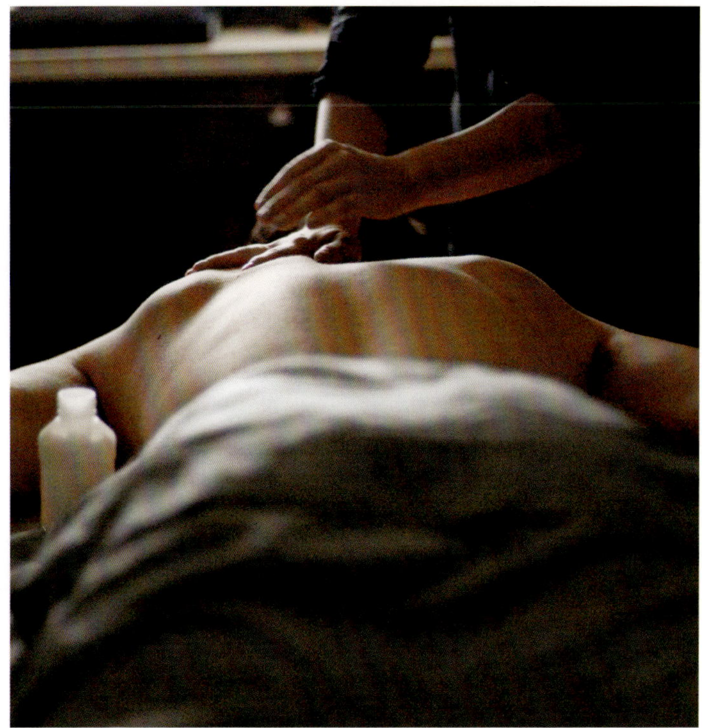

Chicago

New York City

Out to dinner with the crew in Arizona.

In flight hospitality.

Genevieve shares a smile with Chani and friends, Trisha Mears and Jeff Gordon.

Relaxing with friends, Angie Harmon and Jason Sehorn.

Chad pitches in during dinner.

Dinner time at the motorhome lot.

Evening at Talladega Superspeedway.

New Hampshire Motor Speedway

It's pretty rare for one race car driver to say something nice to another one. But at Homestead-Miami in the season finale, during the rain delay, Jeff Burton went out of his way to approach me. He said some of the nicest things anyone has ever said to me in my life. He complimented my driving ability and told me I did a great job representing our sport over the last five years. He said I wouldn't win a sixth championship on this day, but I had nothing to be ashamed of and needed to be proud of all I had accomplished. This moment meant more to me than I can say.

Ron and I go way back, even before NASCAR – all the way back to my ASA days in 1998.

Chad Knaus and our team engineer, Greg Ives (right) observing a practice run.

Hendrick
TEAM LOWE'S RACING
48

Late in the season with Chad Knaus and Greg Ives (left) in our transporter.

I held an event for my team before the 2011 Chase and made a video about the five-straight championships we won. We had an amazing run together and it's always really fun to go back and relive it; to remember how we got there and how rare it is to have been there. We have great camaraderie on our team. That's one of my favorite parts about this business; the time with my guys.

I love this picture of my Crew Chief, Chad, sweeping the floor.

The Lowe's transporter.

Close friends Jason Sehorn and Chip Shelton (on right page).

At Chip Shelton's house with Chip's daughter, Parker, Genevieve and the Shelton's dog, Honey.

Taking a picture of Chani before leaving a restaurant in Texas.

Charlotte Motor Speedway shooting a Time Warner Cable commercial.

VICTORY LANE
dalejr.com
facebook.com/dietdew
diet mtn Dew
NATIONAL
GUARD
dalejr.com
facebook.com/dietdew
diet mtn Dew
NATIONAL
GUARD
GOODYEAR
Holley
HP CARBS

Interviews from Victory Lane in Kansas.

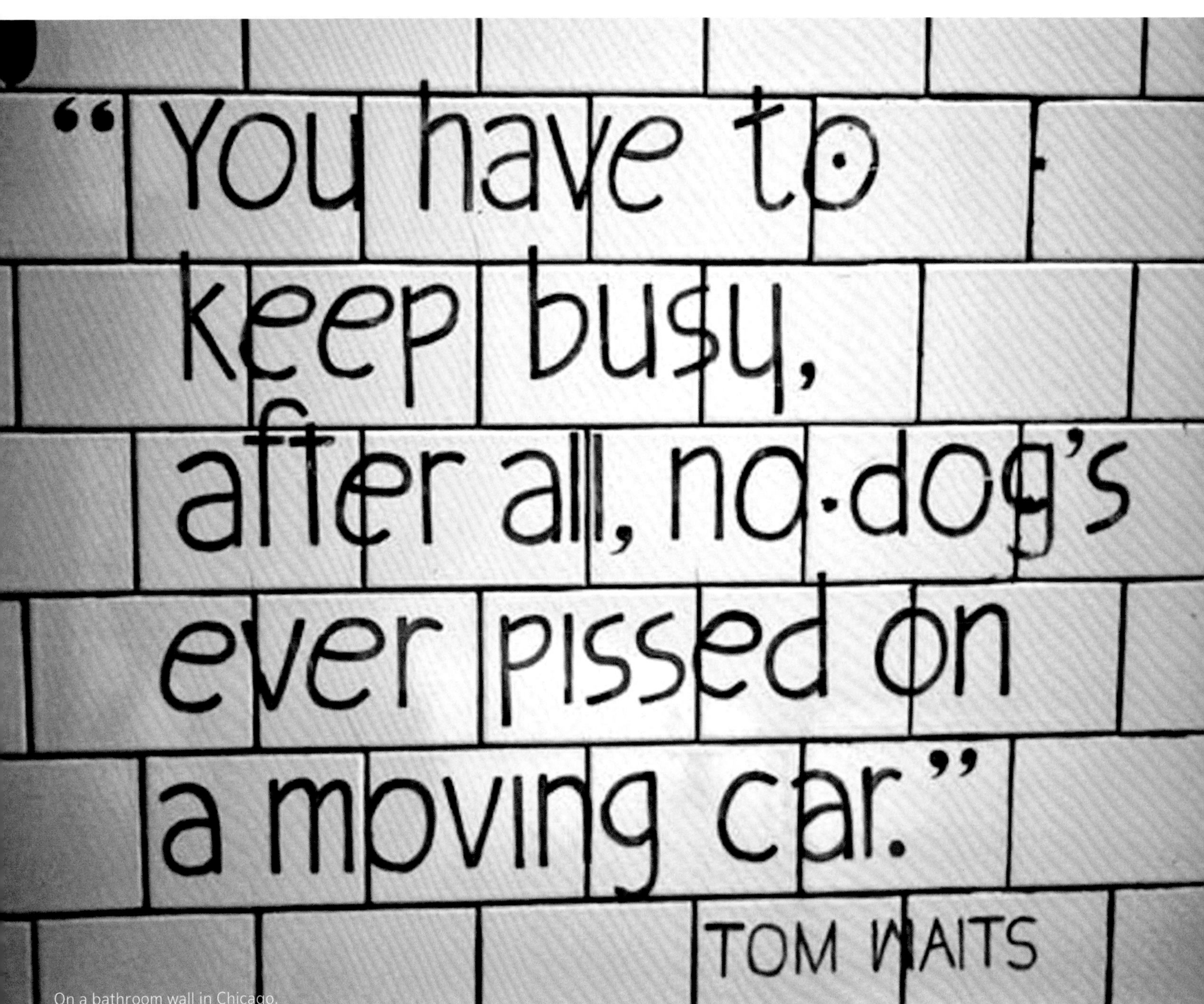

On a bathroom wall in Chicago.

Family pets, Maya and Boxie.

Lowe's Racing

Saying goodnight before a race.

In Muskogee, Okla. for a school event. Chani's childhood friend, Annie Czaruk, is holding Genevieve.

I'm on the other side of the paper, preparing to blast through at a pep rally at Byron Nelson High School in Texas.

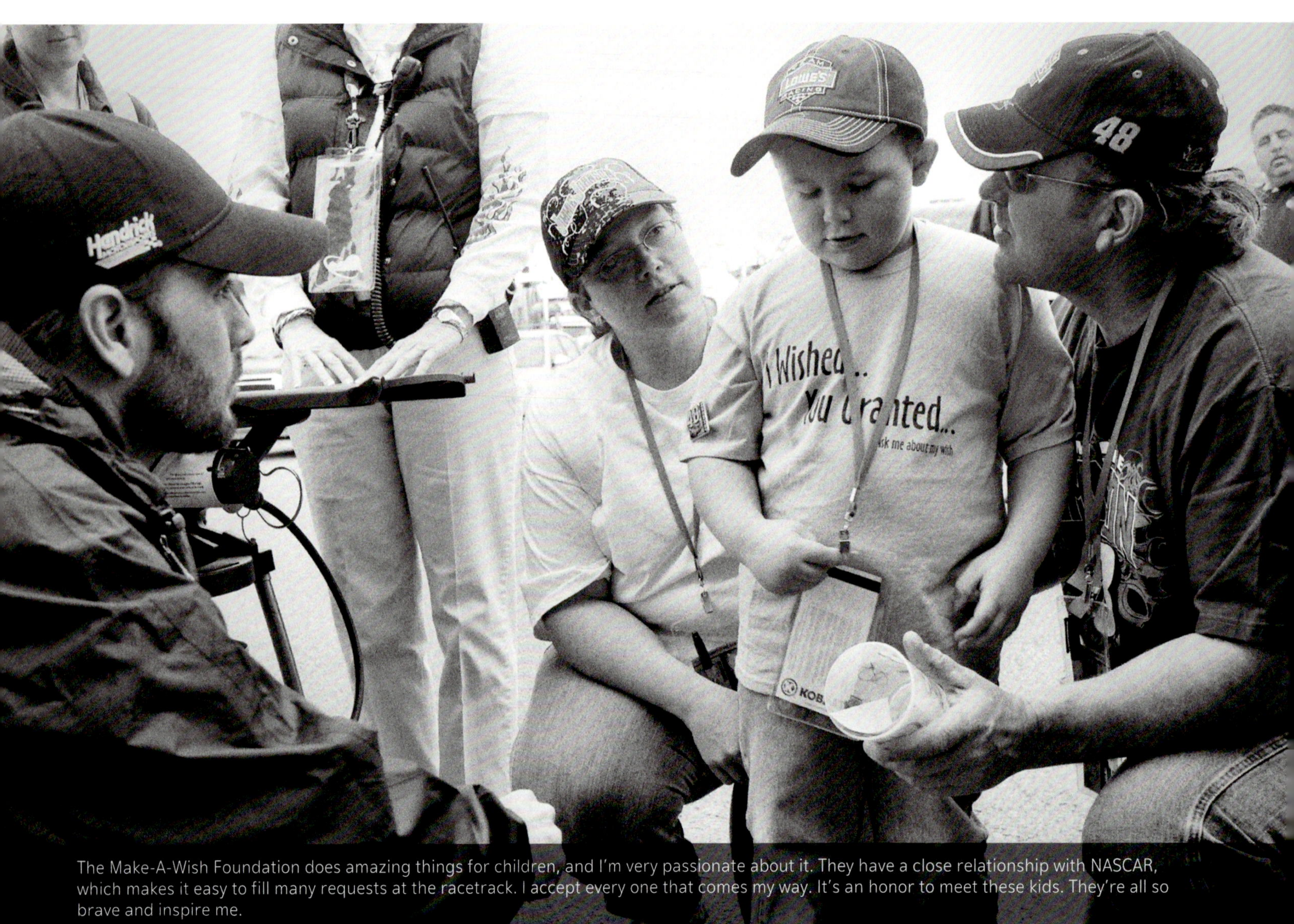

The Make-A-Wish Foundation does amazing things for children, and I'm very passionate about it. They have a close relationship with NASCAR, which makes it easy to fill many requests at the racetrack. I accept every one that comes my way. It's an honor to meet these kids. They're all so brave and inspire me.

"IT'S HUMBLING THAT A CHILD'S LAST WISH IS TO MEET ME."

Signing autographs at an event in Chicago.

Texas Motor Speedway

48
TYRRELL
lowesracing.com
LOWE'S
Let's Build Something Togeth
TEAGUE
lowesracing.com
LOWE'S
Let's Build Something Together

The crew readies for a pit stop.

LOWE'S
RACING
LOWE'S
Let's Build Something Together
Sprint

A good luck kiss from Mrs. Johnson.

LOWE'S
Purolator.
BOSCH
SIEMENS
FREIGHTLINER
LOWES

The motorhome lot is full of kids these days.

A field trip to a pumpkin patch while on the road.

Chani's idea of horsepower – I'm not thrilled.

Apple picking.

At Talladega, wearing a helmet in honor of Dan Wheldon.

Victory Lane at Kansas.

Finishing up Victory Lane in Kansas with Genevieve.

Victory Lane interviews.

A very happy 48 team.

LOWE'S
KOBALT
TOOLS
48
KOBALT
TOOLS
LOWE'S
Jimmie Johnson

Dover International Speedway

A fan camp.

Checking tire wear at New Hampshire Motor Speedway.

A bro hug in post race inspection at Kansas with my race engineer, Greg Ives (brothers gotta hug)!

This shows just how long the team is around after a win, no other transporter in sight.

Go Jimmie !!

mylowes
IMPALA
48
GOODYEAR
Gatorback BELTS
MOOG
MAHLE
COMP
Edelbrock

Back to work.

2012 AND BEYOND

After racing for a decade at NASCAR's highest level and traveling extensively around the country, I still feel like I'm just getting warmed up. With every new year comes new rewards and new challenges, and I'm fortunate to be part of a sport that has provided me a career filled with both. For as long as I can remember, racing has been the number one priority in my life. I had to scrape and claw to get here and received a lot of valuable (and necessary) help from a lot of people along the way. I will always appreciate that and never forget it.

Racing will always be a priority for me, and I will continue to make the necessary sacrifices to achieve my goals of winning races and championships. My desire to be the best racecar driver alive burns as hot as ever. It's no different now than it was racing off road trucks as a teenager. But family is first now. Being the best husband and father I can possibly be is very important to me and fulfills me unlike even winning can.

I am also very passionate about the work Chani and I do through the Jimmie Johnson Foundation. We've seen the impact it has had on schools, charities and families across the country, and we're humbled by it. We're so blessed and if we can make a wish come true for a sick child, or help a school or area in need, we will do everything in our power to contribute.

This book is a passion project for Chani and me. We hope you've enjoyed this glimpse into our lives as much as we enjoyed sharing it. And this is just the beginning. I will continue to share information about my career through my website:

JIMMIEJOHNSON.COM

MISSY MCLAMB

I am not a sports photographer and before the 2011 Chase for the NASCAR Sprint Cup the only thing I knew about stock-car racing was that it required a lot of left turns. But Chandra trusted my vision as an artist, and Jimmie trusted Chandra.

I watched how the veteran track photographers captured the race with the command and skill that only comes from decades of practice. Instead of trying to imitate what they had perfected, I chose to document the races the same way I would photograph the more private and intimate moments of Jimmie's life. Quietly, slowly—and with simple tools.

With the exception of my Leica M9 which is digital, I used all film cameras, most of them medium format, sometimes I even hauled out a 4x5 Graflex view camera. Film and medium format cameras (Rolleiflex, Holga, Diana and Mamiya 7) are slower than 35mm and require me to change the film after 12 exposures. But the limits of my equipment forced me to anticipate, to watch, to learn and to feel the action. At first, I relied on the track radio to understand what was happening during the race, but eventually I learned to watch the crew, the fans and Jimmie's body language. Oftentimes I would only fire one frame as Jimmie zoomed by. I watched and waited for the light, the composition and the car.

The strength of the 48 team reveals itself in the infield of the track, the edge of the track is where Jimmie takes the most risks, Victory Lane is where he collects his paycheck, and inside the motorhome is where he retreats to a secure, calm family. Chandra, his stalwart partner, lover and best friend, possesses the kind of beauty that seems fantastical when you first meet her. Very quickly, however, the force of her physical beauty relents and allows her intelligence, curiosity and openness to fill the space around Jimmie.

What struck me most about Jimmie was is his fervent belief in balance. It's as if he has an internal mechanism that adjusts his mind and body. Just when you think the pressure and speed will force him to the edge—he resets that inner gear.

To bear witness and document the "everyday" within these extraordinary lives has been a whirlwind. I hope as a fan of NASCAR, a fan of Jimmie's, or simply a fan of photography you find not only pictures of a sport, a celebrated athlete, or a beautiful family; I hope these photographs reveal the humanity of a man whose values, loyalty and kindness have created a life worth celebrating. I will be forever in he and Chandra's debt for allowing me inside their world.

PLATES

Page 5: Jimmie and Chani
Page 6: Jimmie, Chani, Genevieve at Martinsville.
Page 10-11: Halfway through The Chase, (left) Victory Lane at Kansas Speedway.
Page 12-13: My team celebrating our victory at Kansas Speedway.
Page 14: Jimmie
Page 15: How Kansas Victory Lane looked from my vantage point.
Page 16-17: Kansas Speedway
Page 18: Tearing up the lawn during my victory celebration at Kansas.
Page 19: Marc Puchalski making adjustments during practice.
Page 20: Rain delay at Homestead-Miami Speedway.
Page 22-23: My walk to qualifying at Charlotte Motor Speedway (I'm talking my right foot into staying on the gas).
Page 24: Jimmie in his Lowe's helmet.
Page 25: Mechanic underneath the Lowe's Chevy.
Page 26: Waking up to the magic number, 48.
Page 27: One last shot before I roll out to practice in Martinsville.
Page 28: A brief moment of downtime between pre-Chase events in Chicago.
Page 29: Family time.
Page 30: Bubble contest with Genevieve.
Page 31: My Girls. I'm a blessed man!
Page 32: New Hampshire Motor Speedway
Page 33: Taking a stroll through the Chicago motorhome lot with Genevieve.
Page 34: Team Lowe's Racing at New Hampshire.
Page 35: Charlotte Motor Speedway
Page 36-37: Story time.
Page 38: Home away from home—our motorhome kitchen.
Page 39: Genevieve, Chandra and Jimmie.
Page 40: Chandra and I walking the red carpet at the BeLive Gala in South Beach, a charity event held by our friends Connie and Juan Pablo Montoya to raise awareness for challenges in their home country of Columbia.
Page 41: Following the BeLive Gala, we are headed to dinner in South Beach with our friend and fellow driver Brian Vickers.
Page 42-43 Martinsville Motor Speedway, (lr)Chatting with the boss – Rick Hendrick.
Page 44-45: Dover International Speedway
Page 46: Bart Apple (l) and (r) Marc Puchalski
Page 47: SportsCenter interview.
Page 48: Celebrating at Kansas Speedway.
Page 49: Talladega Superspeedway
Page 50-51: Byron Nelson High School pep rally.
Page 52-53: Young fans enjoying Foundation Fest—a Jimmie Johnson Foundation event in Charlotte.
Page 54: Media event prior to The Chase.
Page 55: Media event, Victory Lane at Kansas, another media event, Dover International Speedway.
Page 56: Sports Illustrated cover (pre-Chase)
Page 57: Firesuits Dale Jr. and I wore during a commercial shoot for Time Warner Cable in Charlotte.
Page 58 - 59: Sharing a laugh with Dale Jr. between takes.
Page 60-61: The 2012 Team Lowe's Racing photo shoot.
Page 62: Doing an interview for ESPN from Victory Lane in Kansas.
Page 63: Homeward bound.
Page 65: Genevieve enjoying the ride home with Dad.
Page 66: Genevieve, Chani and Jimmie.
Page 67: Juggling work and home.
Page 68: Preparing the BoDeans set list for Jimmie Jam Chicago.
Page 69: Relaxing at a Jimmie Jam event.
Page 70: On stage at Jimmie Jam Chicago with musician and friend Edwin McCain.
Page 71: At the House of Blues Chicago.
Page 72-73: On stage with Los Lobos. On my left is friend and driver Adrian Fernandez.
Page 74-75: Chani receives the Key to the City of Muskogee by Mayor John Hammons for her philanthropic work with the Jimmie Johnson Foundation while Genevieve peeks from backstage.
Page 76-78: Loyal fans.
Page 79: The smallest member of the crew.
Page 80: The prerace prayer.
Page 81: Homestead-Miami Speedway
Page 82-83: Charlotte Motor Speedway
Page 84-85: The Charlotte Motor Speedway crash.
Page 86-87: In Talladega six days after the crash.
Page 88: Jimmie's helmet honoring Dan Wheldon.
Page 89: Watching news coverage of Wheldon's crash.
Page 90: A family moment.
Page 91: Between practice runs at Phoenix International Raceway.
Page 92: Jimmie completing the Outing Report and analyzing data.
Page 93: Crew Chief Chad Knaus
Page 94: Talladega Superspeedway
Page 95: A fan at Talladega Superspeedway.
Page 96-97: Chad Knaus and Jimmie.
Page 98: Texas Motor Speedway
Page 99: Phoenix International Raceway
Page 100: CenterStage with Michael Kay, Yes Network.
Page 101: ESPN's NASCAR Now studio.
Page 102: Production room of the YES Network.
Page 103: Hannah Storm and Jimmie on-set at ESPN's SportsCenter studio.
Page 104: New York City
Page 105: On my way to Late Night with Jimmy Fallon, New York City.
Page 106: In the green room with Jimmy Fallon and my buddy, Doug Keith.
Page 107: Late Night with Jimmy Fallon.
Page 108: Lowe's crew.
Page 109: New Hampshire Motor Superspeedway
Page 110: Strapping in for a practice run.
Page 111: Chatting with Chad in the team transporter. His face tells me we are clearly not having a good day on the track.

Page 112: Talladega Superspeedway
Page 113: Signing autographs on the way back to the transporter.
Page 114-115: Fans
Page 116: John Vignona, our motorhome driver, and Genevieve on our golf cart.
Page 117: A fan at Talladega.
Page 118: Talladega Superspeedway
Page 119: A prayer at the end of a driver's meeting.
Page 120-121: Fans at Talladega.
Page 122-123: Fans
Page 124: Fans on the racetrack during driver introductions at Charlotte Motor Speedway.
Page 125: This was a first for me: I was asked to Homecoming by a student during a pep rally at Bryan Nelson High School in Texas.
Page 126-127: Loyal fans in any weather.
Page 128-129: Pit road under caution at Texas Motor Speedway
Page 130-131: Crew getting the Lowe's Chevy ready for post race inspection.
Page 132: At Homestead-Miami during the rain delay talking to the crew guys.
Page 133: The crew pushing the car to post race inspection at Texas Motor Speedway.
Page 134: Chandra and Genevieve.
Page 135: Phoenix International Raceway
Page 136: Chatting with Car Chief, Ron Malec.
Page 137: Pit road at Dover International Speedway.
Page 138: New Hampshire Motor Speedway
Page 139: Final restart at the Kansas Speedway
Page 140: Prerace at the Kansas Speedway.
Page 141: Talladega Superspeedway
Page 142: Stretching before the race.
Page 143: Working out and massage.
Page 144: Chicago
Page 145: New York City
Page 146-147: Out to dinner with the crew in Arizona.
Page 148: In flight hospitality.
Page 149: Genevieve shares a smile with Chani and friends, Trisha Mears and Jeff Gordon.
Page 150: Relaxing with friends, Angie Harmon and Jason Sehorn.
Page 151: Chad pitches in during dinner.
Page 152: Dinner time at the motorhome lot.
Page 153: Evening at Talladega Superspeedway.
Page 154: New Hampshire Motor Speedway
Page 155: Fan Q&A event.
Page 156: Jeff Burton talks with Jimmie during the rain delay at Homestead-Miami Speedway.
Page 157: Ron and I go way back, even before NASCAR – all the way back to my ASA days in 1998.
Page 158-159: Chad Knaus and our team engineer, Greg Ives (right) observing a practice run.
Page 160: Late in the season with Chad Knaus and Greg Ives (left) in our transporter.
Page 161: 48 team event before the 2011 Chase.
Page 162: I love this picture of my Crew Chief, Chad, sweeping the floor.
Page 163: The Lowe's transporter.
Page 164-165: Close friends Jason Sehorn (l) and Chip Shelton (r).
Page 166: At Chip Shelton's house with Chip's daughter, Parker, Genevieve and the Shelton's dog, Honey.
Page 167: Taking a picture of Chani before leaving a restaurant in Texas.
Page 168-169: Chandra and Jimmie together.
Page 170-171: Jimmie Johnson
Page 172-173: Charlotte Motor Speedway doing a Time Warner Cable commercial.
Page 174: Interviews from Victory Lane in Kansas.
Page 175: On a bathroom wall in Chicago.
Page 176: Traveling
Page 177: At the airport.
Page 178-179: Saying goodnight before a race.
Page 180: In Muskogee, Okla. for a school event. Chani's childhood friend, Annie Czaruk, is holding Genevieve.
Page 181: I'm on the other side of the paper, preparing to blast through at a pep rally at Byron Nelson High School in Texas.
Page 182: A wish request for Make-A-Wish.
Page 183: Signing autographs at an event in Chicago.
Page 184: Texas Motor Speedway
Page 185-186: The crew prepares for pit stops.
Page 187: Jackman TJ Ford drying the pit box.
Page 188-189: A good luck kiss from Mrs. Johnson.
Page 190: Motorhome life (tl) Jamie McMurray's wife, Christy, and their son, Carter; (tr) A field trip to a pumpkin patch while on the road. (ll) Chani's idea of horsepower – I'm not thrilled.
Page 191: At Talladega, wearing a helmet in honor of Dan Wheldon.
Page 192: Victory Lane at Kansas.
Page 193: Finishing up Victory Lane in Kansas with Genevieve.
Page 194-195: Victory Lane (Kansas).
Page 196-197: Dover International Speedway
Page 198: A fan camp at Talladega Superspeedway.
Page 199: Checking tire wear at New Hampshire Motor Speedway.
Page 200: A bro hug in post race inspection at Kansas with my race engineer, Greg Ives (brothers gotta hug)!
Page 201: This shows just how long the team is around after a win, no other transporter in sight.
Page 202: A fan writes "Go Jimmie!!" on the pit road wall.
Page 203: Back to work.

SPECIAL THANKS

To our family and friends for their love, friendship and support. To Missy McLamb, for investing the time, effort and care to ensure the images captured our life. To Mark Pollard and Sylvia and Steve Weir, for taking our vision and making it into this amazing book.To Lance Armstrong, for the idea to do this project. To Marty Smith, for providing insight and perspective that helped shape the message. To everyone at Hendrick Motorsports and our partners, for embracing this project and allowing the access necessary to really give fans a glimpse into our lives.